JUNIOR PET CARE

KITTENS

Photography Susan Miller
Hugh Nicholas
Illustration Robert McAulay
Reading and Child Psychology Consultant
Dr. David Lewis

ACKNOWLEDGMENTS

With special thanks to Mrs. Lang,
Mrs. Cherry Walters and Mrs. Antonia Williams;
Menor Photographic Services;
Jenny Toft, Pet Bowl.

Junior Pet Care

Guinea Pigs
Hamsters
Kittens
Parakeets
Puppies
Rabbits
Snakes
Turtles

This edition © 1990 TFH Publications, Inc., 1 TFH Plaza, Neptune City, NJ 07753. This special library bound edition is made expressly for Chelsea House Publishers, a division of Main Line Book Company.

1 3 5 7 9 8 6 4 2

Library of Congress Cataloging-Publication Data applied for.

ISBN 0-7910-4906-X

CIP

CONTENTS

NOTE TO PARENTS

Cuddly and playful, kittens are enchanting first pets for a child. Kittens are very adaptable but have special needs and need some special care. ***KITTENS*** has been written for children of age 7 years and older to enable them to understand and care for their new kitten.

You and Your Kitten

Having a kitten is a lot of fun. Kittens are very loving and clever animals. You will notice that they learn new things quickly. When kittens grow up into adult cats, they become more independent, so looking after them will not take up as much of your time. Unlike dogs, cats do not need to be taken out for walks because they can be trained to use a toilet tray.

But you have to give a kitten plenty of your attention by stroking, cuddling and playing with it as much as possible. Kittens learn how to behave by playing, so playing with their owner is an especially important part of growing up.

When you take your new kitten home you are really taking the place of its playful brothers, sisters and mother. A kitten will spend hours playing on its own or with another cat but it particularly enjoys a game with its new owner.

All kittens are different in nature. Just like people, kittens have varying likes and dislikes and they all have their own individual personalities. The more attention you give your kit-

ten right from the start, the closer the bond between you will grow and you will soon get to know each other well.

A cat is not a toy that you can put aside if you become bored with it. Besides feeding your cat twice every day and playing with it, you will have to be prepared to arrange for someone to look after it when you go away on vacation.

Some cats can live to be 14 years old, so when you buy your kitten you

are taking in a very big responsibility for a long time in the future.

The more you play with your kitten, the easier it will be for both of you to get to know and appreciate each other. A kitten's needs are similar to your own—children need to play with other children or brothers and sisters and enjoy the attention of their mother or father, too.

Buying a Kitten

Once you are sure that a kitten is the right pet for you, you must decide what kind of kitten you would like. Most kittens are **cross-bred** kittens. This means that their parents probably had different characteristics—different coat colors, for example.

A **purebred** kitten will grow up to be a known size, shape, and color because its parents both belonged to a particular breed. There are lots of different breeds of purebred cats.

The kinds of kittens

Longhair kittens have a long, soft, silky coat. The most popular of the longhaired cats are the **Persians.** If you do decide to buy a longhair kitten you must be prepared to spend some time every day grooming it.

Shorthair kittens have short, dense fur. The most popular of the

Longhair kittens (below) have a gentle nature and come in plenty of different coat colors.

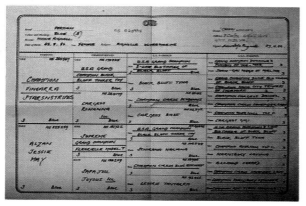

The breed certificate with the family tree of the blue longhair (left) is shown here.

shorthaired cats are the **Siamese** and the **Abyssinians.**

Most full-grown cats, whether shorthaired or longhaired, have greenish-yellow eyes, but some have blue or brown eyes. Some cats even have eyes that don't match in color. The color of a kitten's eyes can change as it grows older.

A black British shorthair (above) and a tabby shorthair (right). They are tough and sturdy cats with a calm and affectionate nature.

Choosing your kitten
You can buy your new kitten from a local pet store. When you go to the pet store, look at the kittens carefully. A mother cat usually has between 3 and 5 kittens at one time and all together they are called a **litter**.

A personal choice
When you go to the pet store to buy your new kitten you will probably see all the kittens in a litter playing happily together. You can tell quite a bit about what a kitten will be like when it grows up just by watching it carefully while it plays with its mother and brother and sisters.

Whatever kind of kitten you choose, you can be sure that your kitten will provide endless hours of enjoyment.

You might notice that one of the kittens is more shy than the others. It will try to avoid being handled and may be smaller and weaker than its littermates. This kind of kitten is called the **runt**. It is not a good idea to choose this one as your pet because it may well grow up to be a timid, weak cat and perhaps remain unfriendly towards people.

Another kitten in the litter may appear to be more fierce than the oth-

If you buy two kittens, their play-fighting may appear rough, but they are not likely to hurt each other.

ers. It may scratch for no reason when you try to pick it up or snarl and hiss at its littermates. This kind of kitten will probably not make a good pet either.

If you can, pick a bold and playful kitten, one that is lively and eager to come to you and explore what is going on. The kitten that seems to be the most naturally alert, friendly and playful will probably adapt well to its new home and make a wonderful pet.

The age to buy a kitten

Kittens are usually ready to leave their mother and go to their new home when they are about eight weeks old.

Buying two friends

If your kitten is going to be left on its own in the house a lot, it might be wise for you to buy two kittens. They can grow up and play together. They will also keep each other company

and will not be lonely while you are out at school all day.

A healthy kitten

There are several signs of good health to look for when you pick out your kitten.

The **body** should be rounded and plump and not feel skinny or bony.

The **eyes** should be bright and clear.

The **nose** should be dry and not runny. If you notice the kitten sneezing, with runny eyes and runny nose,

it might already have a cold, so it is best not to pick this one.

The **ears** should be clean. If there are dark, gray patches in the kitten's ears, it might have ear mites.

The **coat** should be free from fleas. These are very tiny—about the size of a pinhead. If a kitten does have fleas, the black flea will show up better on a light-colored coat. If you are looking at a cross-bred kitten, remember that if it has a fluffy coat, it will almost certainly grow up to be a longhaired cat.

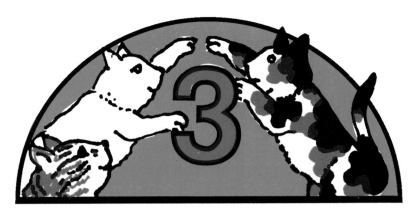

Preparing for
a New Kitten

A cardboard carrier for your kitten will not last long.

A more sturdy kind of kitten carrier.

Before you bring your kitten home, it is best to visit a pet store and make sure you have bought everything your kitten will need to settle into its new home.

First of all, a carrying basket is very useful to take your new kitten home in. There are different kinds available in pet stores. The ones that look like a cardboard box are fine for a short journey but they are not very strong and will only last for one or two trips.

A sturdier and longer-lasting kind of carrier is a wicker basket with a wire mesh front. You might need it to take your kitten to the veterinarian for a check-up. Whatever kind of container you choose, make sure that it fastens securely, has air holes and is lined with newspaper.

Your kitten's bed

You can buy all different kinds of cozy beds for kittens from pet stores. Some are specially made so that they can be cleaned easily. You can even buy ones with built-in heaters.

Toilet trays with or without lids are available from your pet store.

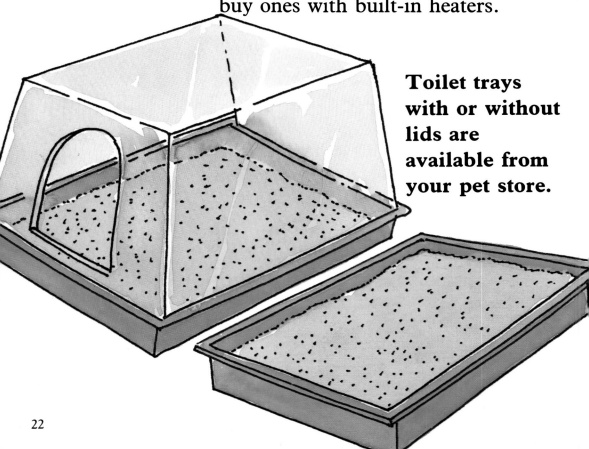

A toilet tray

This is essential for a kitten for the first few weeks, until it is old enough to be able to go outdoors on its own. A toilet tray will of course be essential for your kitten if you live in an apartment or a busy area where it could be dangerous to let your cat outdoors. The tray will need to have low sides so that the kitten can climb in. It is best to buy a plastic tray which is easy to clean. You will find a good choice available at your pet store.

Half-fill the tray with special cat litter, which you can also buy from a pet store. Put the tray in a quiet corner or near the door to the yard. You should change the litter often as kittens are such clean animals that they

will not use a tray that smells. Always wash your hands afterwards.

Cat flap

Pet stores sell neat, draft-proof cat flaps and it is a good idea to buy one, especially if you and your family are out during the day. You will need to ask an adult to fit it into the back door.

Having a cat flap will allow your kitten to go in and out whenever it wants. Your kitten will soon learn to go out instead of using a toilet tray.

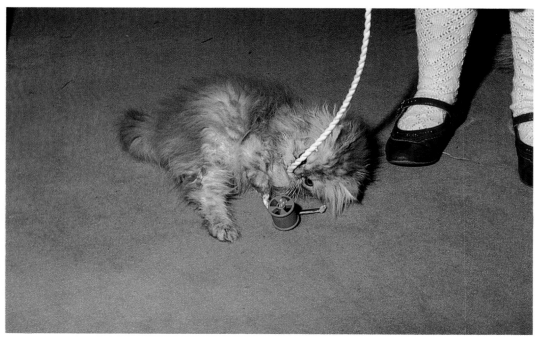

Toys

You can buy special toys for your kitten from pet stores. They might even have **catnip**. Catnip is a plant that has strongly scented leaves. Kittens and cats love the smell. It makes them very excited and even more playful than usual. If you grow some catnip in your garden you will have great fun watching your kitten romping and enjoying itself.

Kittens often like the most simple toys. A kitten will be entertained with an old wooden spool or a ping pong ball for hours. If you encourage

An indoor scratching post (above right) and an outdoor one—a tree (above).

your kitten to play, you will both have lots and lots of fun.

Scratching post

Cats will often sharpen their claws on furniture. To prevent your new kitten from ruining your parents' furniture, it is often a good idea to buy a scratching post. You can train the kitten to use the post by moving its paws up and down it a few times.

Settling in

A young kitten that has just left its mother and brothers and sisters might be very shy and homesick at first.

Some kittens like to be on their own for a while in a quiet place until they get used to their new home. Don't worry; in a few days your pet will start to feel more confident and playful.

Kittens love attention and a kitten's personality develops more if it is handled and played with. You should always be gentle when handling a kitten.

Feeding Your Kitten

When you first buy your kitten, ask what the kitten has been used to eating, how often it is fed and how much. Begin feeding your kitten in the same way for the first few days until it has settled in. Then you can introduce changes and new foods gradually.

To make sure your kitten grows into a healthy adult cat you will need to give it the right kinds of foods. In

the wild, a kitten would mainly eat what its mother had caught—small animals like birds and mice. Pet cats are still natural meat-eaters. Kittens also need to have meat in their diet in order to grow up and remain healthy.

Milk

There is no question that milk is a nourishing food. It contains **calcium,** a mineral which helps to make teeth and bones grow and keeps them healthy and strong.

However, some kittens, and even some adult cats, cannot digest milk, and it can cause their stomachs to become upset.

Your veterinarian can recommend other foods that contain calcium and that will be easier for your kittens to digest.

Kittens use their tongue to lap up liquids—it becomes spoon-shaped.

Prepared food

Most of the specially-prepared canned or dried food for kittens that you can buy in pet stores contain all

the correct kinds of ingredients for your kitten.

Using canned or dried food is the simplest way of feeding and most kittens and cats are quite happy to eat it. They will soon let you know what flavor they like best. If a cat or kitten does not like the kind of food you are feeding it, it usually refuses to eat it.

Remember that, just like us, kittens do like to try different kinds of food and have favorite treats too. If

If you feed your kitten milk, it may upset his stomach.

you use dry food, make sure that your kitten has plenty of water available to drink.

Feeding times

With a young kitten under 12 weeks old, it is best to give it four meals a day. The size of each meal should be small—only about one tablespoon of food. From 12 weeks onwards, your kitten can go down to three meals a day and by the age of six to seven months, two meals a day are enough. As you give your kitten fewer meals, you must put a little more food in each meal.

Some cats like to find their own water, but if it is unclean it can make them sick.

Your kitten's diet should include fresh meat and dried (or canned) kitten food.

All kittens are different. Some are much greedier than others and some grow more quickly, so you can vary these rules to suit your special kitten. If your kitten leaves food, you might be giving it too much to eat. Or, the opposite could be happening. You might find your kitten mewing for more to eat if you are not giving it enough.

Do not be alarmed if you see your kitten chewing on grass. Grass is sometimes good for cats because it helps them bring up fur swallowed when grooming. Also, it provides cats with **roughage.** This is like bran for

Exploring the big wide world is an exciting experience for a kitten, but it can also be dangerous.

people—we have roughage from foods like cereal, whole wheat bread and fruits and vegetables. If your kitten is not allowed outdoors, it is best to grow some grass for it in a pot indoors and keep it by your kitten's water bowl.

Fresh food

A kitten will probably appreciate being offered some fresh food. Kittens like meat—rabbit, heart, liver, chicken. They like fish too. Make sure that an adult has cooked the food first and that it has cooled before giving it to your kitten. Also, check that there are no bones in any fish or chicken that you feed to your kitten. Even small bones can get stuck in your kitten's throat.

Kittens do not need to have fresh meat every day. They only need it as an occasional treat—for one or two meals a week. If you do feed your kitten mainly fresh food, you must include some cereal. The kind of cereals that kittens need are already mixed into prepared kitten foods.

Cats can be like little lions and may try and catch other pets like hamsters.

If its adult teeth have come through, the kitten will be more than seven months old. You can tell the age of a kitten by looking at its teeth (below).

You may also use a vitamin and mineral supplement which is available from pet stores.

A kitten's teeth

Kittens have only "baby" teeth until they are about seven months old. As their teeth are small at first, it is best to chop or mince any meat or fish finely, to make it easier for your kitten to chew. Crunchy dried cat food is good for a kitten's teeth.

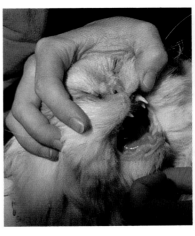

Training
and Behavior

A kitten's mother usually teaches it to do basic things like how to drink milk out of a saucer and how to use the toilet tray. When your kitten arrives at your house, you will be taking the place of its mother, teaching it how to behave and what it is allowed and not allowed to do.

Kittens are very responsive and learn new rules quickly. A kitten will understand what you mean by the way you treat it and the tone of your voice. Praise your kitten when it does

Kittens and cats love to play with small objects. They use their sensitive paw pads to move their toys.

the right thing. On the other hand, if it is naughty, you should scold it in your firmest voice, as though you really mean it. Your kitten will understand that you are angry simply by the sound of your voice.

Naming your kitten

You will need to think of a name for your new kitten if it does not already have one. Choose a short name that is easy to say and recognize. Call your

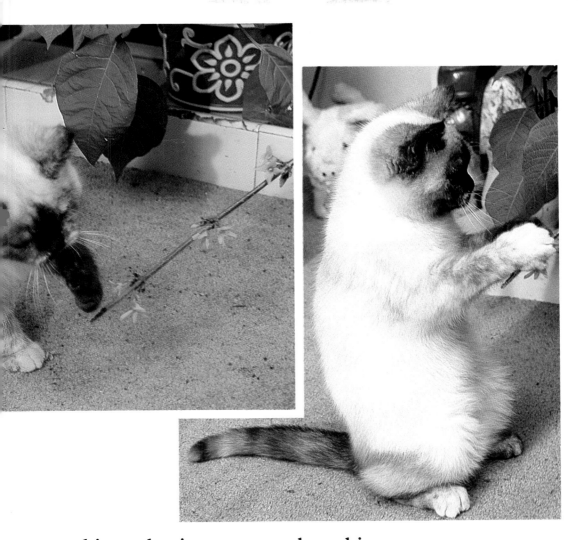

new kitten by its name or by whistling or clicking your tongue. When it comes to you, give it a big hug to show how pleased you are. Many kittens soon recognize their owners' footsteps or even the sound of their car. Your kitten might well run to meet you when you come home.

Sometimes cats groom themselves when they are nervous or frightened.

Learning new rules

It is important to make firm rules for your kitten right from the start, as soon as you bring it home. Kittens are very clever animals and learn fast. But you must be consistent. If you let your kitten do something one day and not the next, it will become confused.

Decide where in the house your kitten is allowed to go. For example, most people do not let their kitten jump up onto kitchen worktops, or onto a stove where it might get burned. Also, decide whether you want to keep your kitten out of any rooms, such as your parents' bedroom. Never let your kitten curl up and go to sleep in a baby's crib or stroller.

It is important to keep to the rules you have made. Kittens are mischievous—which makes them fun to be with. They are like children in that they might try and be naughty just to see if you let them get away with it.

It is natural for kittens to jump up

GROOMING YOUR KITTEN

First wipe the kitten's face.

Use a metal comb to groom the kitten.

Make sure the kitten's ears are clean.

Fluff up the fur and give it an extra shine by plenty of stroking.

A slow blink is a sign of contentment (right). A kitten's ears are erect if the kitten is alert.

on high places, scratch furniture and chase birds. If you do not want your kitten to do these kinds of things, make it clear from the start, with a firm "no." Kittens are sensitive and most of the time they do want to please their owner, so you should be firm but gentle when you are training your kitten.

Using the toilet tray
At first your new kitten might not know where the toilet tray is. Be

A kitten holds its tail high if it feels happy and alert. If you see the tail twitching at the end, it means that the kitten is angry, excited or curious.

ready to pick it up and put it on its toilet tray at the first sign that it might want to go. If you watch your kitten you will soon notice it will start to sniff around looking for a suitable place. This part of having a kitten is a little like potty-training a baby. But cats are very clean animals and do not take long to learn where they are supposed to go.

Praise your kitten when it uses the tray. If your kitten forgets and you see it go elsewhere, scold it firmly and put it on the tray immediately. But there is no point in scolding a kitten for something it has done wrong a while ago, as it will not understand.

If your kitten does make a mess on the floor, you should clean the spot at once with disinfectant. Otherwise the smell will remain and encourage the kitten to go there again. If you have a fenced-in garden you will gradually be able to let your kitten out and it will soon learn to use the garden instead of the toilet tray.

Going out

Most kittens will not venture outdoors into new places on their own until they are sure where they are and that they can return home safely. However, a kitten, as well as an adult cat, faces many dangers when it is allowed to roam freely. It can be injured or it can get lost. It is best to allow your kitten to go out into a securely fenced yard where you can watch over him.

A kitten's whiskers are very sensitive to touch and are used to tell how wide a gap is.

PROTECTION FOR YOUR KITTEN

You should take your kitten to the veterinarian to be vaccinated when it is about two months old.

Kittens have a great deal of energy but they do need plenty of sleep, too. Try not to wake your kitten up when it is sleeping.

Understanding your kitten

Cats do have a language and if you listen carefully, you will be able to understand your kitten's little soft sounds. When kittens purr it means that they are happy. Sometimes they make other gentle sounds which may be a greeting to you. Most cats do make a few definite sounds you will soon learn to interpret as meaning "in" or "out" or "feed me."

Health care
for your kitten

Kittens and cats can catch illnesses just as we do and if you think your kitten is ill, the best thing to do is ask a grown-up to help you to take it to see a veterinarian.

Vaccinations

Soon after you get your kitten, take it to a veterinarian so that it can be vaccinated. This is an injection to prevent your kitten from catching **cat flu.** Cat flu is a serious disease that can affect cats that have not been vaccinated against it. A rabies vaccination may also be necessary depending on where you live. The veterinarian will advise you in this matter.

Hair balls and stomach upsets

Tufts of fur sometimes become stuck in a kitten's throat and it can cough and splutter for a while with this problem. Kittens can often provide their own remedy, if they are let outdoors, by eating grass. If your kitten is sick repeatedly, it is best to take it to a veterinarian.

Ear problems

A kitten's ears are extremely delicate. You should never poke anything, not even your fingers, in your kitten's ear. If your kitten or cat shakes its head in pain and scratches its ear, take it to see a veterinarian. A grass seed or thorn may be lodged in the kitten's ear. Another common cause of ear trouble is an ear mite. This is a tiny animal that lives in the wax, deep down in the kitten's ear.

Eye problems

If your kitten's eye is swollen, partly closed or weepy, you should take it to a veterinarian for treatment. Kittens have a "third eyelid" which looks like a film across the surface of the eye. If your kitten is ill, you might notice this.

Fleas

Sometimes even the best kept kitten might have fleas. If you do find some fleas on your kitten, sprinkle your kitten carefully with a special cat flea powder, sold in pet stores. If this does not work, ask your veterinarian for a more powerful flea spray but be careful and ask a grown-up for assistance when de-fleaing a kitten. When you have treated the kitten, you also need to wash the kitten's bedding and vacuum the house thoroughly to destroy any flea eggs.

Worms

Kittens can catch roundworm from their mother, and this may make them less active than normal. Cats can also catch another kind of worm, tapeworm, from fleas or rats. If you think your kitten is suffering from worms, take it to see a veterinarian for treatment. It is a good idea to talk about this when you take the kitten for its first vaccination.

Glossary

Calcium A very important part of a kitten's diet, as it helps his bones grow strong and hard. A main source of calcium is milk.

Catnip A plant whose scent, when put into cat toys, makes both kittens and cats more playful and excited than usual.

Cross-bred A kitten is called a cross-bred when its parents are each different breeds.

Ear mite A tiny animal that lives in a kitten's ear, causing itchiness and pain.

Longhair kittens Distinguished by longer, softer coats, their bodies are generally shorter and stockier than shorthair kittens.

Orientals Another name for foreign kittens and cats.

Pedigreed A kitten with parents of the same breed. Pedigreed kittens will grow up to look much like their parents.

Persians A purebred breed of kitten with long hair.

Roughage A type of food necessary for kittens and cats, as it aids in the digestive process. For example, a kitten may chew on grass as a form of roughage.

Runt The smallest and weakest of the litter. For health reasons, it is generally not a good idea to choose the runt of the litter for a pet.

Shorthair kittens Distinguished from kittens of the longhaired breeds by having shorter hair and (generally) a more slender body. Siamese and Abyssinian kittens, for example, are shorthaired cats.

Index